Foreword

Each show garden at the Royal Horticultural Society (RHS) Cl around a theme or concept that engages people and stimulates ic have been sponsored around a particular charitable cause. Th people to connect with the cause often using plants and design to symbolise and spread awareness of the charity's message.

By utilising the show gardens in this way, the charitable message is communicated to visitors spreading knowledge and information as well as providing an opportunity to raise funds for future charitable investments.

RHS Chelsea helps to highlight charitable causes by not only being visited by over 170,000 people in less than one week but also by being covered extensively in the press, in the U.K and around the world.

For the designers, this was a key motivation to create the 'Cavernoma on My Mind Garden'. By taking part in the show, it will throw a much needed spotlight on this rare and little known disease. The garden will remind us all of the fragility of nature as well as human life. It will engage and stimulate our senses and feelings and demonstrate horticulturally the science of nature as a healer. Both the magic and logic of gardens, the art and the science, is captured in the Cavernoma on My Mind Garden design for all of us to enjoy, experience and better understand the work of Cavernoma.

This mindfulness colouring book is part of the Cavernoma story. Colouring is known to be therapeutic for many of us and especially sufferers of certain neurological conditions. The colouring book and the Cavernoma on My Mind Garden aim to help Cavernoma patients by spreading knowledge about the condition, so they feel that they aren't alone and that their particular challenge is understood and can be overcome. This book contributes to their journey.

Keith Weed CBE
The President of the Royal Horticultural Society

From the Designers

Connecting with nature helps us achieve mindfulness. The design and selection of the plants for the Cavernoma on My Mind Garden at the RHS Chelsea Flower Show 2023 rests on the important relationship between nature and cavernoma patients, which is represented in the garden in multiple ways. With this mindfulness colouring book we have highlighted some of the key plants in the garden for you. By purchasing this awareness raising book you are doing your bit for the cavernoma patients and participating in funding this garden.

Nature can be a healer for many people with cavernoma, who go through various periods of hardship with varying degrees of severity. Even a single plant can have an impact on well-being and support a healing process.

For example, the beauty of peonies (*Paeonia officionalis* and *lactiflora*) in the garden awakens positive feelings but they are also a part of this garden for their root extract's remarkable medicinal qualities against epilepsy and seizures. Yarrow is a hardy plant, which survives even in the toughest of places. Unfortunately, it is an often overlooked plant. Cowslip brings the smile in people's faces after the winter, being bright yellow and *Rosa* 'Nuits de Young' denote the despair and fear of death that cavernoma sufferers feel. Cornflowers, these beautiful blue flowers used to be very common seen in rye fields. Foxgloves are very toxic to humans, but parts of the plants are used for medicines against heart failure. Poppy is a symbol of Remembrance and hope for a peaceful future. Of course, the garden would not be the same without raspberries, because their looks are used to describe how a cavernoma looks and that also explains the raspberry on our cover page. Thistles' prickles remind about the kind of stinging pain the cavernoma patients feel. The dark flowers of African lily's (*Agapanthus* 'Black magic') flowers symbolise the darkest moments felt by cavernoma patients and their families. Woodland Sage, healthy food is crucial for humans. Sages have multiple medicinal uses. Lily of the Valley' is the National Flower of Finland. It's lovely scent in spring brings back memories from the childhood. The plant is highly poisonous. *Malus* 'Peter's Red' is at the RHS Chelsea Flower Show for the first time ever. Red flowers will symbolise the fact that cavernoma is a condition related to abnormalities in blood vessels.

The pictures of the plants used in the Cavernoma on My Mind Garden have been named by using English common names as well as the Finnish ones. Plants in this Cavernoma on My Mind Garden can be grown in different countries and Cavernoma touches people around the world.

On the map of the garden, you will find the plants numbered in the areas where they will be used. That way, we hope, you will get a deeper connection with the Cavernoma on My Mind Garden. In the book there will be a full plant list and map with marked areas where the plants are located.

1 in 625 people in the UK are estimated to have a brain cavernoma without symptoms, with a symptomatic cavernoma being much rarer. It's therefore important to raise awareness of this condition, not only so that members feel less alone, but in order to advance treatment, research, and support for those affected. In United Kindom there are two charities supporting cavernoma patients and their families: Cavernoma Allience, cavernoma.org.uk and Cavernoma Society, cavernomasociety.org.uk.

Flowery regards

Taina Suonio and Anne Hamilton

Cavernoma on My Mind Garden
RHS Chelsea Flower Show

The Cavernoma on My Mind Garden features at the RHS Chelsea Flower Show in 2023 and it is designed to help raise awareness of cavernoma globally, but to also depict the feelings, sensations, and journey that a cavernoma patient goes through – helping them to feel heard and understood. The condition is rare and often the patient is more of an expert when it comes to their symptoms and struggles than the doctors and surgeons.

Mainly sponsored, and designed by Chelsea favourite Taina Suonio and her designer colleague Anne Hamilton, the garden is divided into sections – each depicting and evoking feelings or symptoms that are common amongst patients with cavernoma, such as Fragility of Life, Unconditional Love, and a Fresh Start.

Acer griseum, commonly known as blood-bark maple, recalls the thin blood vessels of cavernomas and its peeling bark symbolises the fragility of life. *Taxus baccata* cushions in different sizes represent the stages of cavernoma with the prickly foliage echoing the shooting nerve pains that patients suffer from. The dark flowers of *Rosa* 'Nuits de Young' and *Agapanthus* 'Black Magic' denote the despair and fear of death that cavernoma patients feel. Raspberries also feature in the garden for their physical resemblance to cavernoma.

Above the planting, glass steps ascend to a viewing platform and a water feature which flows gently down a wall, completing the garden.

Designers will invite surgeons, neurologists, and patients to the garden to share their experiences and learn from one another. The garden will hopefully be donated to a neurological hospital after the show.

13
5
12
3
9
2
7
6
8
1
11
4
10

For what it's worth, it's never too late to be whoever you want to be. I hope you live a life you're proud of, and if you find you're not, I hope you have the strength to start over.

– F. Scott Fitzgerald

1 Peony Pioni

Mindfulness gives you time.
Time gives you choices. Choices,
skilfully made, lead to freedom.

– Bhante Henepola Gunaratana

2 Yarrow Siankärsämö

How we pay attention to the present moment largely determines the character of our experience, and therefore, the quality of our lives.

– Sam Harris

Cowslip Kevätesikko

Happiness, not in another place but this place...
not for another hour, but this hour.

– Walt Whitman

Rose Ruusu

Be happy in the moment.
That is enough.

– Mother Teresa

5 Cornflower Ruiskaunokki

Sometimes the bad things that happen in our lives put us directly on the path to the best things that will ever happen to us.

– F. Scott Fitzgerald

Foxglove Sormustinkukka

Believe you can, and you're halfway there.

– Theodore Roosevelt

7 Poppy Unikko

The mind is like water.
When it's turbulent, it's difficult to see.
When it's calm, everything becomes clear.

– Prasad Mahes

Raspberry Vadelma

Surrender to what is.
Let go of what was.
Have faith in what will be.

– Sonia Ricotti

9 Thistle Ohdake

Nature does not hurry,
yet everything is accomplished.

– Lao Tzu

African Lily Sinisarja

Each morning we are born again.
What we do today is what matters most.

– Buddha

11 Woodland Sage Salvia

*Begin doing what you want to do now.
We are not living in eternity. We have only this
moment, sparkling like a star in our hand
melting like a snowflake.*

– Francis Bacon Sr.

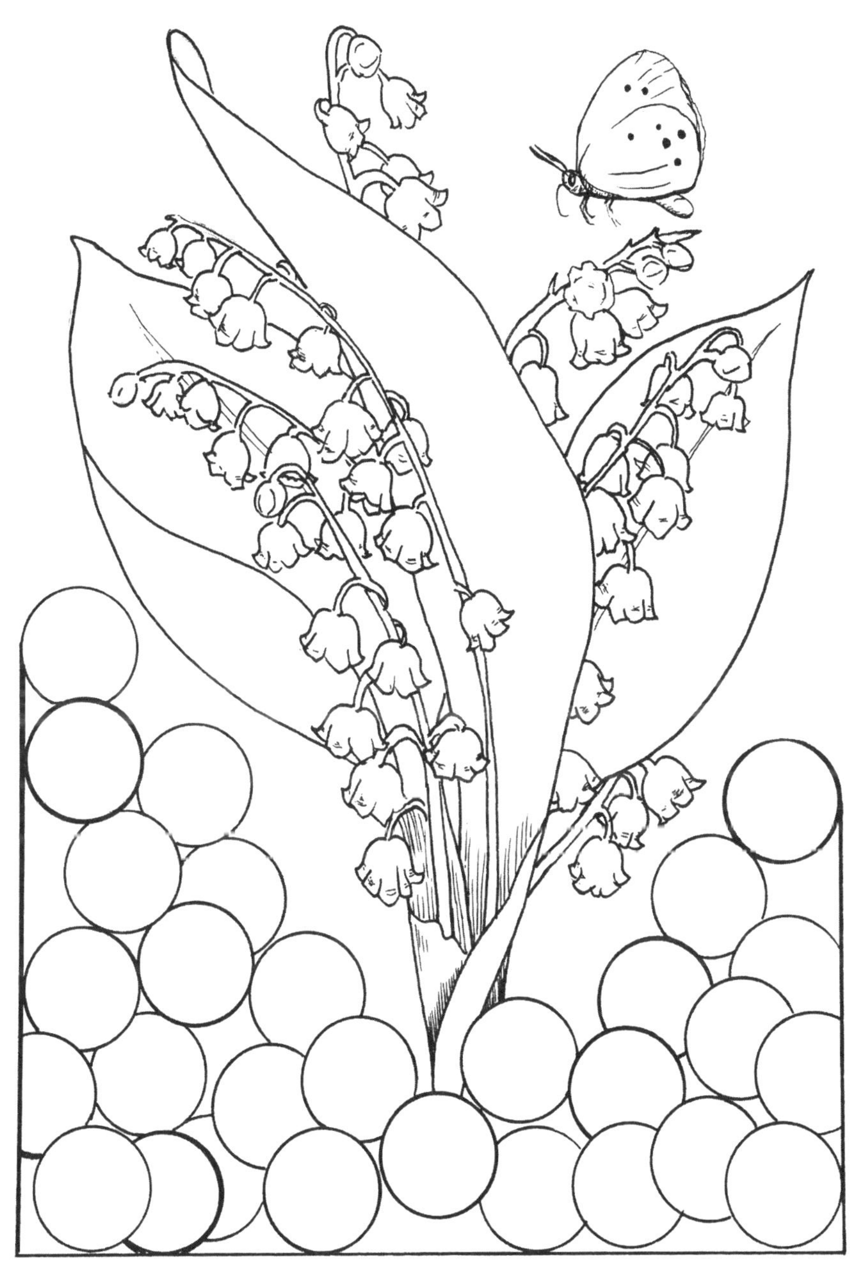

 Lily of the Valley Kielo

Some days are better; some days are worse.
Look for the blessing instead of the curse.
Be positive, stay strong and get enough rest.
You can't do it all, but you can do your best.

– Doe Zantamata

 Malus 'Peter's Red' Omena

About the Designers

Taina Suonio

Taina is an internationally awarded landscape designer, horticulturist, MSc. environmental biologist and researcher in the Fifth Dimension - Vegetated Roofs in Urban Areas research group of the University of Helsinki. Her research concentrates particularly on the environmental change and policy regarding vegetated roofs in urban areas.

This will be Taina's 18th year at Chelsea and her fourth garden. Her style of garden design is foremost a celebration of the natural, ecological biodiversity supporting beauty of the native wild, without forgetting a touch of the more dashing elements of flowering glory in carefully selected areas of her designs. Taina has designed gardens, roof gardens, vegetated roofs and parks in the UK, China, and her native Finland and she is a member of a design team for a major project in Japan.

Anne Hamilton

Whilst Anne has worked on Chelsea gardens for many years, this will be her first garden as a designer at the Show.

Based in Ireland since 2007, she has been working in the field of garden design for more than 20 years and has designed gardens in Ireland, the UK, USA and Spain. Most of Anne's work is for private clients, but she's also worked in conjunction with the Environmental Protection Agency, Dublin City Council and Bord Gáis, and is currently working on a project for the South Infirmary Hospital Victoria and a local play park. She has previously designed and built two award-winning show gardens at Bloom in the Park, Dublin, Ireland, so she is no stranger to success. At the RHS Chelsea Flower Show she has worked with designers such as Mark Gregory, Nigel Dunnett, Adam Frost and Taina Suonio.

A member of Anne's family has recently been diagnosed with cavernoma, meaning that collaborating on this garden has personal significance for her.

The Team

The garden will be built by Tom Salmon Landscaping Ltd, with support from George Weldon of The Yorkshire Gardener and Krisztian Gyory of GreenFlow.

Illustrations for the book

Contemporary landscape artist Lucy MacQueen is a Londoner based in Texas.

Contact: lucymacqueen.com or @lucymacqueen_art
Her work is also available online at saatchiart.com

Taina Suonio

Anne Hamilton

Lucy MacQueen

A Flowery Thank You!

We would like to thank, first of all, the Royal Horticultural Society (RHS) for giving us this amazing opportunity to create the Cavernoma on My Mind Garden at the RHS Chelsea Flower Show 2023. By doing so You, the RHS, give a voice to the many people who have cavernoma and their close ones.

We are delighted to say that the Foreword is by RHS President Keith Weed CBE, who by raising the profile of charities behind gardens, represents the true RHS Chelsea Flower Show spirit and spurs us all on to create a very special garden for a very special cause, thus connecting us with the people we represent and all of us with the wider world.

Members of the Cavernoma Society – thank you for believing in us. As designers we hope that with the Cavernoma on My Mind Garden we will give you strength and enjoyment alike. This garden is primarily for you and by using flowers, trees and design, it will be your message to the world. We feel that it should reflect all the feelings that you are going through, not shying away from the darker moments and uncertainty that you go through.

There are a couple of people to whom we pay a special tribute for working pro bono to make a reality the Cavernoma on My Mind Garden mindfulness colouring book that you are holding in your hand. Skilled graphic designer Kari Tervo and the artist illustrator, lovely Lucy McQueen, whose elegant drawings brought the book to life – how can we thank you enough!

Without our sponsors we could not complete this garden. We would like to give our SPECIAL THANKS to some of our donors and supporters: BIG Hedge Co, thanks to your kindness the garden has a "framework", which supports wildlife too. We all know how important part the soil plays for the health and well-being of plants and trees. Kekkilä-BVB supplied us environmentally friendly recycled soil, suitable for the different growing areas in the garden. QuadraBuild, we commend you for your generosity for the structural building phase, for your support and kindness Marco Rossi (GL&SS), Nagual Koru Jewellery, Eeva Mela, Pat Morrissey Construction Company LTD, Nangle and Niesen Wholesale Nursery, Steel Landscaping Co., Gardenworld Wholesale Nursery Growers, National Timber Group, Juha Moisio, Ivan Ivanoff, Aaro Suonio, BiodiverCity Oy, Johanna Viheraho, LOKI Suomi Oy/ Anne Paljakka, Murdo Ross, Marja Mesimäki, Nadine Brown, Laura Hinttula, Julia Wallin, Puutarhaliitto ry, Puunkaatopalvelu O & L Oy, Tim Howell, Addagrip Terraco, Lindum, Peter Beales Roses Ltd, Steel Options, Glasstec Systems, Majestic trees, Jouko and Marja Marttila, Deepdale and Timothy Leech, you have all been of great help and an inspiration to us all.

At the time of this book going to print we are not yet in the position to mention and thank all of our dear donors and supporters - companies and individuals, but we hope to see many of you at the show; and for the ones who cannot make it, you can all claim ownership of this important project and let its purposeful story warm your hearts as you follow the evolving story through the media. We hope you love this garden as much as we do. THANK YOU!

A big Thank You goes naturally to our magnificent team: Tom Salmon Landscaping Ltd, Krisztian Gyory of GreenFlow and George Weldon of The Yorkshire Gardener. WE ARE THE TEAM!

Last, but not least, we would like to thank our families for their patience, love and support! This is something we just have to get done!

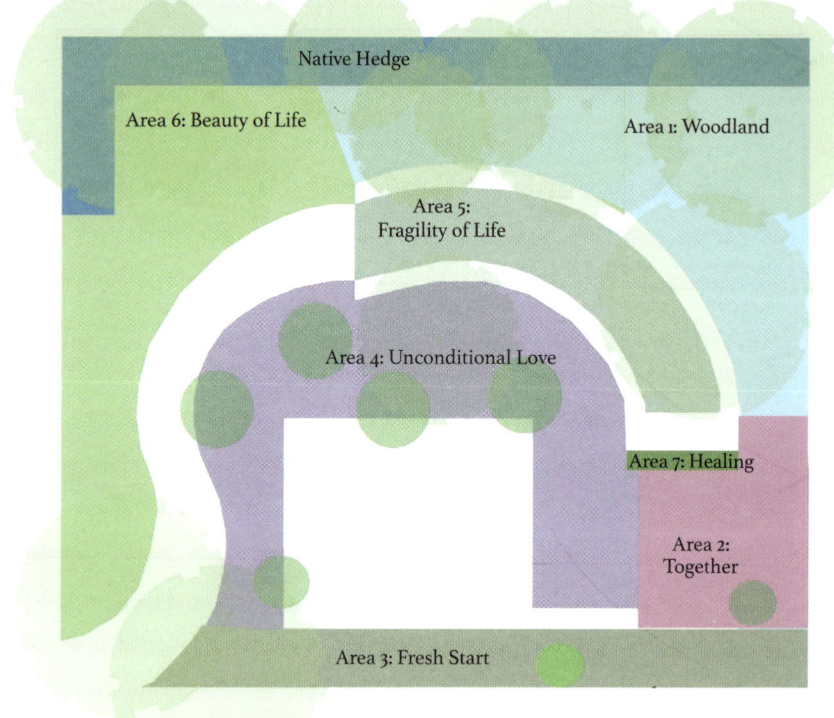

Area 1:
Anthriscus sylvestris *(Cow parsley)*
Centaurea cyanus *(Cornflower)*
Digitalis purpurea *(Foxglove)*
Dryopteris filix-mas *(Fern)*
Festuca ovina
Juniperus communis
Matteuccia struthiopteris
Molinia caerulea *(Purple moor-grass)*
Papaver ssp. *(Poppy)*
Rosa glauca *(Redleaf rose)*
Rubus idaeus *(Raspberry)*
Silene viscaria
Deschampsia flexuosa *(Wavy hair-grass)*
Trifolium pratense
Trifolium repens
Viburnum opulus
Viola tricolour *(Viola)*

Area 2:
Achillea millefolium 'Cerise Queen'
Agastache 'Black Adder' *(Giant hyssop)*
Angelica gigas 'Vicar's Mead'
Angelica gigas 'Ebony'
Artemisia ludoviciana 'Silver Queen' *(Wormwood)*
Lythrum virgatum 'Dropmore Purple'
Mentha spp. *(Mentha piperita 'Swiss')*
Salvia nemorosa 'Merleau Rose'
Shrub Rose 'White Pet'
Shrub Rose 'Comte de Chambord'
Shrub Rose 'Nuits de Young'
Taxus baccata, cushion *(Yew)*
Verbasum 'Dark Eyes'

Area 3:
Agapanthus 'Black Magic' *(African Lily 'Black Magic')*
Artemisia ludoviciana 'Silver Queen'
Festuca ovina
Knautia macedonica *(Widow flower)*
Mentha spp. *(Mentha piperita 'Swiss')*
Oraganium vulgare *(Oregano)*
Paeonia 'Amani' *(Peony 'Amani')*
Paeonia 'Itoh Scarlet Heaven' *(Peony 'Itoh Scarlet Heaven')*
Salvia nemorosa 'Caradonna'
Salvia nermorosa 'Merleau Rose'
Salvia ongispicata x farinacea 'Big Blue'
Taxus baccata, cushion *(Yew)*
Thymus vulgaris *(Thyme)*

Area 4:
Achillea millefolium 'Summer berries' *(Yarrow)*
Achillea millefolium 'Cerise Queen' *(Yarrow)*
Anthriscus sylvestris *(Cow parsley)*
Artemisia ludoviciana 'Silver Queen' *(Wormwood)*
Climber Rose 'Pauls H Musk'
Climber Rose 'Cecile Brunner'
Knautia macedonica *(Widow flower)*
Leucanthemum vulgare *(Oxeye Daisy)*
Salvia nemorosa 'Caradonna'
Salvia nermorosa 'Merleau Rose'
Salvia ongispicata x farinacea 'Big Blue'
Shrub Rose Mutabilis
Shrub Rose 'Our Beth'
Shrub Rose 'Happy Memories'
Shrub Rose 'Queen's Jubilee'
Taxus baccata, cushion *(Yew)*
Thymus serphyllum *(Creeping Thyme)*
Thymus vulgaris *(Common Thyme)*

Area 5:
Circium vulgare *(Thistle)*
Papaver spp. *(Poppy)*
Rubus fructicosus *(Bramble)*
Rubus idaeus *(Raspberry)*
Urtica dioica *(Nettle)*
Vitis Vinifera

Area 6:
Anthriscus sylvestris *(Cow parsley)*
Bellis perennis *(Daisy lawn)*
Centaura cyanus *(Cornflower)*
Ferns spp.
Geranium sylvaticum
Rosa glauca *(Redleaf rose)*
Valeriana officionalis *(Valerian)*

Area 7:
Allium schoenoprasum *(Chives)*
Anethum graveolens *(Dill)*
Artemisia ludoviciana 'Silver Queen' *(Wormwood)*
Basilius *(Basil)*
Fragarua x ananassa *(Strawberry)*
Matriccaria chamomilla *(Chamomile)*
Melissa officionalis *(Lemon balm)*
Metha sp. *(Mint)*
Petroselinum crispum *(Parsley)*
Salvia sp. *(Sage)*
Viola tricolour *(Viola)*

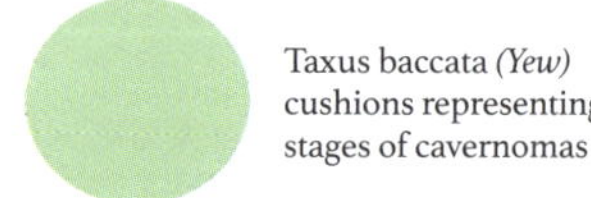
Taxus baccata *(Yew)* cushions representing stages of cavernomas